Saints
CHRONICLES
Collection 2

SOPHIA INSTITUTE PRESS
Manchester, NH

SOPHIA
INSTITUTE PRESS

Text and Images Copyright © 2018 Sophia Institute

Printed in the United States of America.

Sophia Institute Press®
Box 5284, Manchester, NH 03108
1-800-888-9344
www.SophiaInstitute.com
Sophia Institute Press® is a registered trademark of Sophia Institute.

Names, persons, places, and incidents featured in this publication are based on historical fact but have been subject to author and artist discretion for dramatic purposes. All text, except when specifically cited, has been written by the author, not to be mistaken for actual historical documentation.

The Saints Chronicles Collection 1, ISBN: 9781622826742
The Saints Chronicles Collection 2, ISBN: 9781622826766
The Saints Chronicles Collection 3, ISBN: 9781622826797
The Saints Chronicles Collection 4, ISBN: 9781622826803

Library of Congress Cataloging-in-Publication Data

Title: The saints chronicles. Collection 1. Saint Patrick, Saint Jerome
  Emiliani, Saint Elizabeth Ann Seton, Saint Henry Morse, Saint Joan of Arc.
Description: Manchester, NH : Sophia Institute Press, [2018]
Identifiers: LCCN 2018038952 | ISBN 9781622826742 (pbk. : alk. paper)
Subjects: LCSH: Christian saints--Biography--Comic books, strips, etc. |
  Christian martyrs--Biography--Comic books, strips, etc. |
  Catholics--Biography--Comic books, strips, etc. | Patrick, Saint, 373?-463?
  --Comic books, strips, etc. | Jerome Emiliani, Saint, 1486-1537
  --Comic books, strips, etc. | Seton, Elizabeth Ann, Saint, 1774-1821
  --Comic books, strips, etc. | Morse, Henry, Saint, 1595-1645
  --Comic books, strips, etc. | Joan, of Arc, Saint, 1412-1431
  --Comic books, strips, etc. | Graphic novels.
Classification: LCC BX4655.3 .S255 2018 | DDC 282.092/2 [B] --dc23
LC record available at https://lccn.loc.gov/2018038952

THE Saints CHRONICLES

Collection 2

Saint Nicholas.................................. 2
Saint Francis of Assisi.................24
Saint Brigid of Ireland................46
Saint Pachomius...........................68
Saint Anne Line............................90

How do you give to those in need?

Saint Nicholas

Today, the legend and works of St. Nicholas live on through a more familiar face—Santa Claus. However, the man who lived during the third century was much more than a jolly old man in a red and white suit. His compassion and care for all was legendary. After his death on December 6, 343, he was buried in his cathedral church, and this day became known as St. Nicholas Day.

Nicholas is the patron saint of many kinds of people. Sailors look up to him for safety at sea. Brides love him for helping their wedding days go smoothly. Most importantly, St. Nicholas is the special friend of children, protecting them from harm and helping them in times of trouble.

Throughout time, he has been one of the most popular saints with over one thousand churches being dedicated in his honor. He is best known as a worker of miracles and benefactor of the poor. Throughout a life of hard work and good deeds, his faith was unshakable.

This is his story.

Producer Daniel Burton

Editorial Kimberly Black

Story Terry Collins

Line Art Sergio Cariello

Colors Daniel Burton

Letters / Design Jeff Dawidowski

Additional Design Adam Buechler

IN THE TIME OF THE ROMAN EMPEROR CONSTANTINE, TROOPS WERE SENT TO VARIOUS PARTS OF THE EMPIRE TO RESTORE ORDER.

ONE DAY, THE SOLDIERS LANDED IN MYRA, AWAITING CLEAR WEATHER TO CONTINUE THEIR JOURNEY TO PHYRGIA.

THE GENERALS IN CHARGE GAVE THE MEN FREE REIN TO BUY SUPPLIES AND ENJOY DRY LAND BENEATH THEIR FEET.

BUT THE TROOPS WERE WEARY AFTER MANY WEEKS AT SEA AND TOOK THEIR FRUSTRATION OUT ON THE SELLERS IN THE MARKETPLACE.

AN ARGUMENT LED TO A FIGHT BETWEEN THE MERCHANTS OF MYRA AND THE VISITORS.

FEARING FOR THEIR LIVES AGAINST TRAINED SOLDIERS, AND FRIGHTENED A RIOT MIGHT SPREAD INTO THE CITY, THE OFFICIALS AT MYRA SUMMONED BISHOP NICHOLAS TO HELP CALM THE SCENE.

NICHOLAS WASTED NO TIME WITH THE MEN. INSTEAD, HE SOUGHT OUT THEIR COMMANDERS.

Generals, what **violence** have you brought to us here in Myra?

Myra is but a port of call, good Bishop. **Ours** is a peaceful mission to restore order in **Phyrgia**.

Then how is it the **peacemakers** are striking up **trouble** in our town?

Trouble? What trouble do you speak of?

You -- you are the trouble! Your own **soldiers** are looting the market!

THE GENERALS HURRIED OFF TO THE MARKET WHERE THEY PUNISHED THE GUILTY SOLDIERS, COMMANDING THEM TO APOLOGIZE FOR WHAT THEY HAD DONE AND PAY FOR WHAT THEY HAD DESTROYED.

AFTERWARDS, NICHOLAS ATE WITH THE GENERALS AND BLESSED THEM AND THEIR JOURNEY.

HIS WORK DONE, NICHOLAS BEGAN THE LONG WALK BACK TOWARD THE CITY ONLY TO FIND HIS WORK WAS JUST BEGINNING....

Good woman of Myra, why do you **weep**? The soldiers are leaving us in peace. There's nothing --

I **weep** not for soldiers, Bishop Nicholas. I cry for the **deaths** of three innocent men.

Prefect Eustathios accepted a **bribe** and condemned my husband and his brothers to be **slain** at once.

But they have committed **no crime**, other than angering a neighbor.

If you had been here, these **innocent** men would not have been handed over to **death**.

I see -- our chief judge has **overstepped** his authority. There is yet time; take me to where they are to be **executed!**

AS BISHOP NICHOLAS RACED INTO THE CITY, THE EXECUTIONS WERE UNDERWAY.

... And with the **authority** granted to me by the **emperor** himself, I hereby sentence these men to **death!**

While Bishop Nicholas did **forgive**, those in Myra could not.

Nicholas was very **wise** and passed no judgment. His heart only held **love**, and evil cannot withstand such light for long.

But **Storyteller**, how did Bishop Nicholas reach sainthood?

Good question, my child. To fully understand the work of St. Nicholas, we must start at the beginning ...

... AND GO BACK TO WHEN NICHOLAS WAS NOT YET A SAINT, BUT MERELY A BOY.

BORN TO WEALTHY PARENTS IN THE VILLAGE OF PATARA, NICHOLAS GREW UP WITHOUT WORRY OR WANT.

ALTHOUGH HIS FAMILY WAS RICH, THEY WERE KIND AND RAISED THEIR SON TO BE DEDICATED TO THE WORD OF GOD.

NICHOLAS'S LIFE WAS ONE OF DEVOTION, FOR HE KNEW HE WAS SURELY BLESSED.

BUT AT THE CUSP OF MANHOOD, TRAGEDY STRUCK. A PLAGUE SWEPT ACROSS THE LAND ...

AND YOUNG NICHOLAS WAS NOW AN ORPHAN. ON HIS OWN IN THE WORLD, HIS HEART WAS HEAVY, AND HE FELT LOST.

THEN THE WORDS OF JESUS CAME TO HIM: "SELL WHAT YOU OWN, AND GIVE THE MONEY TO THE POOR."

UPON HEARING THIS, NICHOLAS REALIZED THAT NONE OF US ARE ALONE, AS LONG AS THE LORD IS THERE.

AS HE GREW, HE DID WHAT CHRIST REQUESTED OF HIM.

HE MINISTERED TO THE SICK AND THE SUFFERING ...

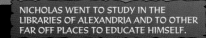

NICHOLAS WENT TO STUDY IN THE LIBRARIES OF ALEXANDRIA AND TO OTHER FAR OFF PLACES TO EDUCATE HIMSELF.

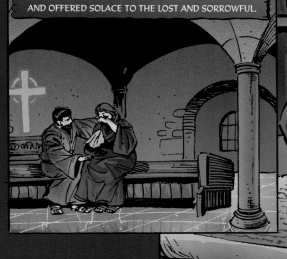

AND OFFERED SOLACE TO THE LOST AND SORROWFUL.

HE THEN RETURNED TO BECOME A MONK IN THE MONASTERY OF HOLY ZION, NEAR MYRA, AND WAS CONTENT TO SERVE IN THAT ROLE.

STILL, HE TOOK GREAT PAINS TO OFFER CHARITY TO THOSE IN NEED. TAKE THE TALE OF THE THREE MAIDENS, FOR EXAMPLE.

To be wed ...

Father, we are old enough ...

Once you have given us our dowry!

THE FATHER OF THE TRIO HAD SUFFERED SEVERAL FINANCIAL SETBACKS. UNBEKNOWNST TO HIS CHILDREN, THERE WAS NO DOWRY TO SEE THEM INTO MARRIAGE.

THE LARGER THE DOWRY, THE BETTER THE CHANCE TO FIND A GOOD HUSBAND. WITH NO MONEY AT ALL, HE FEARED HIS DAUGHTERS WOULD GROW OLD AND LONELY.

AS NICHOLAS HAD THE MEANS TO ASSIST, HE WENT TO THE FATHER'S HOUSE THREE DIFFERENT TIMES, DELIVERING A BAG OF GOLD EACH NIGHT TO SERVE AS DOWRIES FOR THE GIRLS.

Do not **thank** me, good sir. **God** is the one who has answered your prayers.

ON THE THIRD VISIT, THE FATHER CAUGHT NICHOLAS AND PRAISED HIS GENEROSITY. EVER HUMBLE, NICHOLAS ASKED THE MAN TO KEEP HIS ACTS OF KINDNESS A SECRET.

OF COURSE, THE FATHER WAS UNABLE TO CONTAIN HIMSELF, AND THE LEGEND OF NICHOLAS AND HIS COMPASSION FOR THOSE IN NEED CONTINUED TO GROW.

From what I understand, he's been **supporting** the local churches already with his **time**, **money**, and **service**. We might as well make it official.

So, has this **Nicholas** entered the church today?

How can **I** assist today, good Bishops?

Yes, and he waits outside this door. I will **summon** him.

Nicholas, servant and friend of **God**, for your holiness you shall be **bishop** of this place.

I am honored but not **worthy** to be named bishop.

It is not our decision -- it is **God's** will.

Will you guard and protect the **traditions** of the Holy Church and **instruct** the people in your district **in all** matters of the Faith?

I **vow** to bring the **Gospel** of **Christ** to the people and defend the **Faith** from all those who would assail it.

If **God** wills it, I accept the responsibility.

Then sit in the **bishop's** seat and be **ordained**.

BISHOP NICHOLAS WAS TRUE TO HIS WORD AND PERFORMED HIS DUTIES WITH GRACE AND LOVE.

IN ADDITION TO HIS LOCAL DUTIES IN MYRA, BEING A BISHOP CARRIED OTHER RESPONSIBILITIES.

ONE OF THESE WAS HIS PRESENCE AT ALL OFFICIAL CHURCH COUNCILS.

AFTER DAYS OF MEETINGS AND DEBATES, ONE COULD HARDLY BE FAULTED FOR DOZING.

fallen asleep ...

USED TO BEING MORE ACTIVE AND HANDS-ON IN HIS SERVICE TO GOD, NICHOLAS FELT HIS EYES GROW HEAVY.

Bishop Nicholas! Help me!

Eh? I'm sorry ... I must have ...

Later, when the ship arrived safely home, tales of the appearance of Nicholas spread.

Soon, sailors considered him the patron of all travelers of the sea.

Tell the story of how St. Nicholas fed the hungry!

Ah, one of my favorite tales. But you see, he fed them not once, but twice!

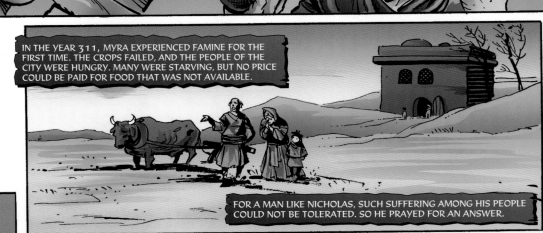

IN THE YEAR 311, MYRA EXPERIENCED FAMINE FOR THE FIRST TIME. THE CROPS FAILED, AND THE PEOPLE OF THE CITY WERE HUNGRY. MANY WERE STARVING, BUT NO PRICE COULD BE PAID FOR FOOD THAT WAS NOT AVAILABLE.

FOR A MAN LIKE NICHOLAS, SUCH SUFFERING AMONG HIS PEOPLE COULD NOT BE TOLERATED. SO HE PRAYED FOR AN ANSWER.

HE FOUND HIS SOLUTION FLOATING IN THE WATERS OF MYRA'S HARBOR.

I'm sorry, Bishop, but we can't spare any of our cargo, not even with you doing the asking.

We've heard of you and your work. You're a **legend** amongst us seafarers.

You've been there for some of us in times of need.

If this were **my** wheat to share, you'd have all you needed and **twice** that.

I **implore** you, sir, to take but one measure of **grain** from each ship so my people will have **food** to ease their **suffering**.

The wheat is weighed and measured, and every bit must be delivered to the emperor.

I cannot spare a cupful ... My own life would be at risk.

Do **this** for me, and I promise, in the name of **God**, that your cargo shall not be **lessened** or diminished when you get to your destination.

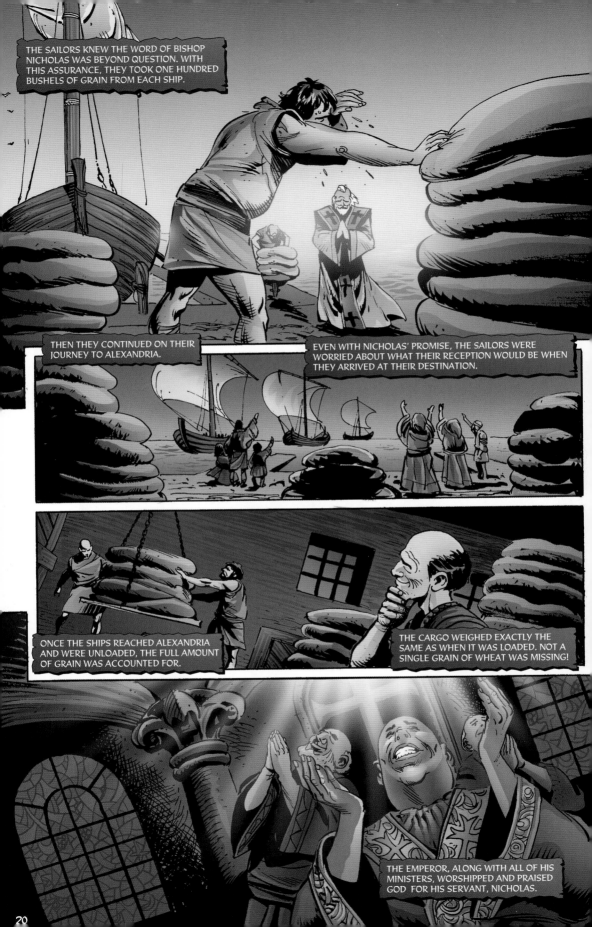

THE SAILORS KNEW THE WORD OF BISHOP NICHOLAS WAS BEYOND QUESTION. WITH THIS ASSURANCE, THEY TOOK ONE HUNDRED BUSHELS OF GRAIN FROM EACH SHIP.

THEN THEY CONTINUED ON THEIR JOURNEY TO ALEXANDRIA.

EVEN WITH NICHOLAS' PROMISE, THE SAILORS WERE WORRIED ABOUT WHAT THEIR RECEPTION WOULD BE WHEN THEY ARRIVED AT THEIR DESTINATION.

ONCE THE SHIPS REACHED ALEXANDRIA AND WERE UNLOADED, THE FULL AMOUNT OF GRAIN WAS ACCOUNTED FOR.

THE CARGO WEIGHED EXACTLY THE SAME AS WHEN IT WAS LOADED. NOT A SINGLE GRAIN OF WHEAT WAS MISSING!

THE EMPEROR, ALONG WITH ALL OF HIS MINISTERS, WORSHIPPED AND PRAISED GOD FOR HIS SERVANT, NICHOLAS.

BACK IN MYRA, BISHOP NICHOLAS WATCHED OVER THE WHEAT GIVEN TO HIM BY THE SHIPS' CAPTAINS.

Take this grain, and distribute it to the four corners of our lands. No one shall go hungry.

THROUGHOUT THE FAMINE, THE PEOPLE CAME TO BISHOP NICHOLAS FOR WHEAT. NO ONE IN NEED WAS TURNED AWAY.

A YEAR PASSED, AND AGAIN, THE SECOND HARVEST WAS STRICKEN WITH BLIGHT.

THE FAMINE LASTED FOR TWO YEARS ...

DURING THE LONG PERIOD WITHOUT CROPS, BISHOP NICHOLAS NEVER RAN OUT OF GRAIN.

THERE WERE WHISPERS OF YET ANOTHER MIRACLE, AS THE SUPPLY WAS ENDLESS.

THE GRAIN LASTED AS LONG AS NEEDED, WITH ENOUGH REMAINING TO PLANT NEW CROPS.

AND THE NEXT YEAR THE GRAIN TOOK SEED, GREW, AND MULTIPLIED.

21

A Saint's Journey

C. 280

NICHOLAS IS BORN DURING THE LATE THIRD CENTURY NEAR THE CITY OF MYRA, A PROVINCE OF ASIA MINOR (WHICH IS NOW KNOWN AS THE COUNTRY OF TURKEY). HE IS BORN TO WEALTHY PARENTS WHO RAISE HIM AS A CHRISTIAN.

NICHOLAS' PARENTS DIE OF DISEASE WHILE HE IS STILL YOUNG. REMEMBERING THEIR WORDS AND THE WORDS OF CHRIST, HE SELLS HIS BELONGINGS AND GIVES THE MONEY TO THE POOR.

AS A YOUNG MAN, HE IS MADE BISHOP OF MYRA, WHERE HE IS WELL-LOVED AND RESPECTED AS A LEADER.

NICHOLAS FIGHTS THE PAGANISM OF THE REGION BY DESTROYING SEVERAL PAGAN TEMPLES, INCLUDING ONE DEDICATED TO THE GREEK GOD ARTEMIS.

C. 303

THE ROMAN EMPEROR, DIOCLETIAN, ORDERS WIDESPREAD PERSECUTION OF CHRISTIANS. ST. NICHOLAS SUFFERS FOR HIS FAITH BUT SURVIVES. HE IS LATER RELEASED AFTER A REGIME CHANGE.

C. 325

NICHOLAS IS A VOCAL PRESENCE AT THE FIRST ECUMENICAL COUNCIL OF NICAEA, HELPING TO PRESERVE THE UNITY OF THE CHURCH DURING A TIME OF TURMOIL.

C. 343

ACCOUNTS DIFFER ON THE EXACT YEAR OF THE DEATH OF NICHOLAS, WHICH OCCURS BETWEEN THE YEARS OF 342 AND 345. THE ANNIVERSARY OF HIS DEATH ON DECEMBER 6 IS NOW CELEBRATED AS ST. NICHOLAS DAY. HE IS OFTEN KNOWN TO PROTECT CHILDREN, DEFEND THE DEFENSELESS, AND SECRETLY GIVE GIFTS TO THOSE IN NEED.

Is your heart open to befriending those who have been rejected?

Saint Francis of Assisi

St. Francis of Assisi is one of the most *well-known* and beloved saints of the Catholic church. A man of *conviction*, joy, and peace, St. Francis of Assisi lived his *life* with passionate devotion to the *Word of God* and *followed* the footsteps of Christ by embracing a *life of poverty.*

Founder of the *Franciscan Order*, St. Francis of Assisi was *admired* during his time. He saw poverty as his *closest companion* and the way to a *Christ-like life*. St. Francis' many companions followed his *example* and relinquished all earthly *possessions* of comfort and wealth to spread the *Gospel* and message of the *Church*. They even began wearing *brown robes*, the clothing of the poorest people, as a *symbol* of their dedication to a *life* of *poverty and simplicity*.

St. Francis' life has been *recorded* by biographers, poets, and writers for centuries. *Dante*, one of the greatest poets in *history*, even mentions St. Francis in his famous epic, *Paradise*. St. Francis authored several writings, including the "Canticle of the Sun," "Rule(s) of the Friars Minor," *"Testament of St. Francis,"* and many *letters* and prayers.

St. Francis was *canonized* in 1228, only *two years* after his death, by *Pope Gregory IX.*

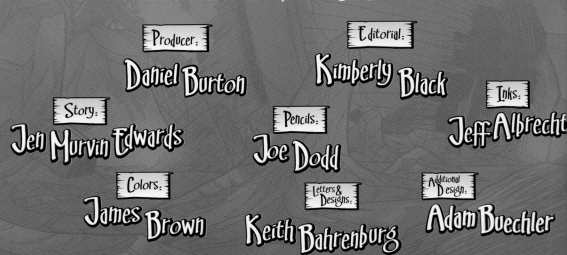

Producer:

Daniel Burton

Editorial:

Kimberly Black

Story:

Jen Murvin Edwards

Pencils:

Joe Dodd

Inks:

Jeff Albrecht

Colors:

James Brown

Letters & Designs:

Keith Bahrenburg

Additional Design:

Adam Buechler

ASSISI, ITALY. 1205: Two Years Later

Well, Francis, *prison* sure didn't *change* you!

It was *two years* ago, Walter, and I've *moved on.* I'm *ready* for bigger and better things *now!*

I hear you desire the life of a *knight!* The Crusades *await!* Or is a life in the *military* too bland for the lively *Francis of Assisi?*

My life is *great*--it's an *endless party.* What's *not* to love? But yes, Walter, I want *more.* Glory! *Recognition! I will go with you!*

SPOLETO, ITALY: *Journey to the Crusades*

LORD, HELP ME!

Please, I'm so sorry ... I never *meant* to forget You ...

Through the years, *Francis* had forgotten how the Lord, In His wisdom and guidance, had *saved* Francis from the sword. But now at night *memories* of prison came to *haunt,* And the Lord chose to remind him of *that* which he forgot.

Francis...

Return to *Assisi,* Francis. You are a *soldier* but *not* in the way you think. Go *back* to *Assisi* where you belong.

I have *strayed* from You, Lord, and yet You *still remember* me. I will do as You *say! I* will go back to *Assisi!*

A few days later.

A *kind* farmer gave me this stone from *his* field. Can you *believe* all of these stones were given *freely* by the people of *Assisi?*

I *do* believe it, *Francis.* After all, *you* were the one that asked them. An *entire* church *rebuilt* by donated stones!

And there's *even* some left over. We could help rebuild *St. Peter's Church* and St. Mary of the Angels as *well!*

How will you find the *time,* Francis? Your ministry with the *lepers takes much* of your day already.

We'll figure it out! Meanwhile, let's *finish* this *wall.* These stones seem to get *heavier by the minute!*

A few days later.

I'm going to *miss* these *woods* while I'm away in Syria. I *always* feel *more* at home in nature than *anywhere* else.

I've heard *many* of the brothers speak of your *love* for *animals* and *nature*.

We are *all* God's creatures.

I have *found* a place for you and your *sister* at a nearby nunnery in *San Damiano*. You will be able to *begin* your work there.

Thank you, Francis.

And may God *bless* you in your *travels*.

GOODBYE, ITALY!

And so **Francis** was on his **way** to preach the **Word** of **God** To those across the **land** and **sea**, to **lonely** souls abroad. As he **left** young **Clare** behind, he had no way to **see** She and **Agnes** would be saints **themselves**, heroes of history.

Francis waved his home **goodbye** on seas as calm as **glass**, But little did he **know**, those **peaceful waters** would **not** last.

Francis' ship was lost before it landed on the shore,
But the men survived, and Francis didn't quit; he wanted more.
His determination could not be quenched by any ocean's squall.
He continued on his travels, bringing the Word of God to all.

For many years he sought to teach peace, love, and poverty.
And while abroad, Francis made Christians of every nationality.

He traveled to Morocco, to Syria and Spain.
Although he soon was taken ill, his efforts were not in vain.

But at home, the **brotherhood** began to bend and **split**. Thousands of men joined the order, but **some** were changing it.

Many Franciscan missions were **established** across the **globe**, But for **Francis the Poor**, as he was known, it was **time** to return home.

ITALY, 1224.

For twenty years Christ encompassed all that Francis sought, And though with time many things had changed, for Francis that did not.

Are you *alright*, Francis? You've seemed quiet these *past few days*.

So *much* has changed, *Brother Leo*. I was happy to give up my *authority* in the brotherhood. I never *really wanted* to be different from my fellow brothers.

I am *humbled* by the *Cross*, this symbol of *Christ's* sacrifice! I am *overwhelmed* by the *sufferings* of our Lord... as if they were *my own* ...

Francis - your hands... *What's happening?*

I- I don't...

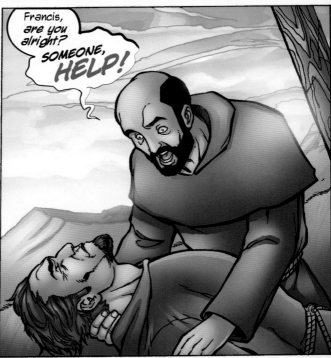

Francis, *are you alright?* SOMEONE, HELP!

FRANCIS BEARS THE WOUNDS OF CHRIST!

42

1226.

Saint Francis preached of love, Of hope, of life in poverty,

"For wealth," he said, "is not Measured in things we see,

But in those things unseen," he said, "Like friendship, love, and prayer."

Even today, Saint Francis' name Is beloved in hearts everywhere.

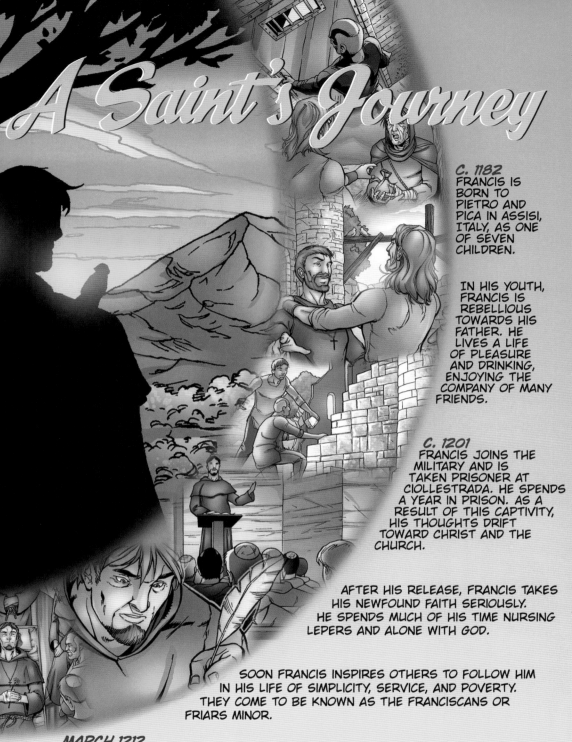

A Saint's Journey

C. 1182
FRANCIS IS BORN TO PIETRO AND PICA IN ASSISI, ITALY, AS ONE OF SEVEN CHILDREN.

IN HIS YOUTH, FRANCIS IS REBELLIOUS TOWARDS HIS FATHER. HE LIVES A LIFE OF PLEASURE AND DRINKING, ENJOYING THE COMPANY OF MANY FRIENDS.

C. 1201
FRANCIS JOINS THE MILITARY AND IS TAKEN PRISONER AT CIOLLESTRADA. HE SPENDS A YEAR IN PRISON. AS A RESULT OF THIS CAPTIVITY, HIS THOUGHTS DRIFT TOWARD CHRIST AND THE CHURCH.

AFTER HIS RELEASE, FRANCIS TAKES HIS NEWFOUND FAITH SERIOUSLY. HE SPENDS MUCH OF HIS TIME NURSING LEPERS AND ALONE WITH GOD.

SOON FRANCIS INSPIRES OTHERS TO FOLLOW HIM IN HIS LIFE OF SIMPLICITY, SERVICE, AND POVERTY. THEY COME TO BE KNOWN AS THE FRANCISCANS OR FRIARS MINOR.

MARCH 1212
FRANCIS ESTABLISHES THE ORDER OF THE POOR DAMES, WHICH WOULD LATER BE CALLED THE POOR CLARES, AFTER CLARE OF ASSISI.

OCTOBER 1226
FRANCIS DIES.

How are you a positive influence in other people's lives?

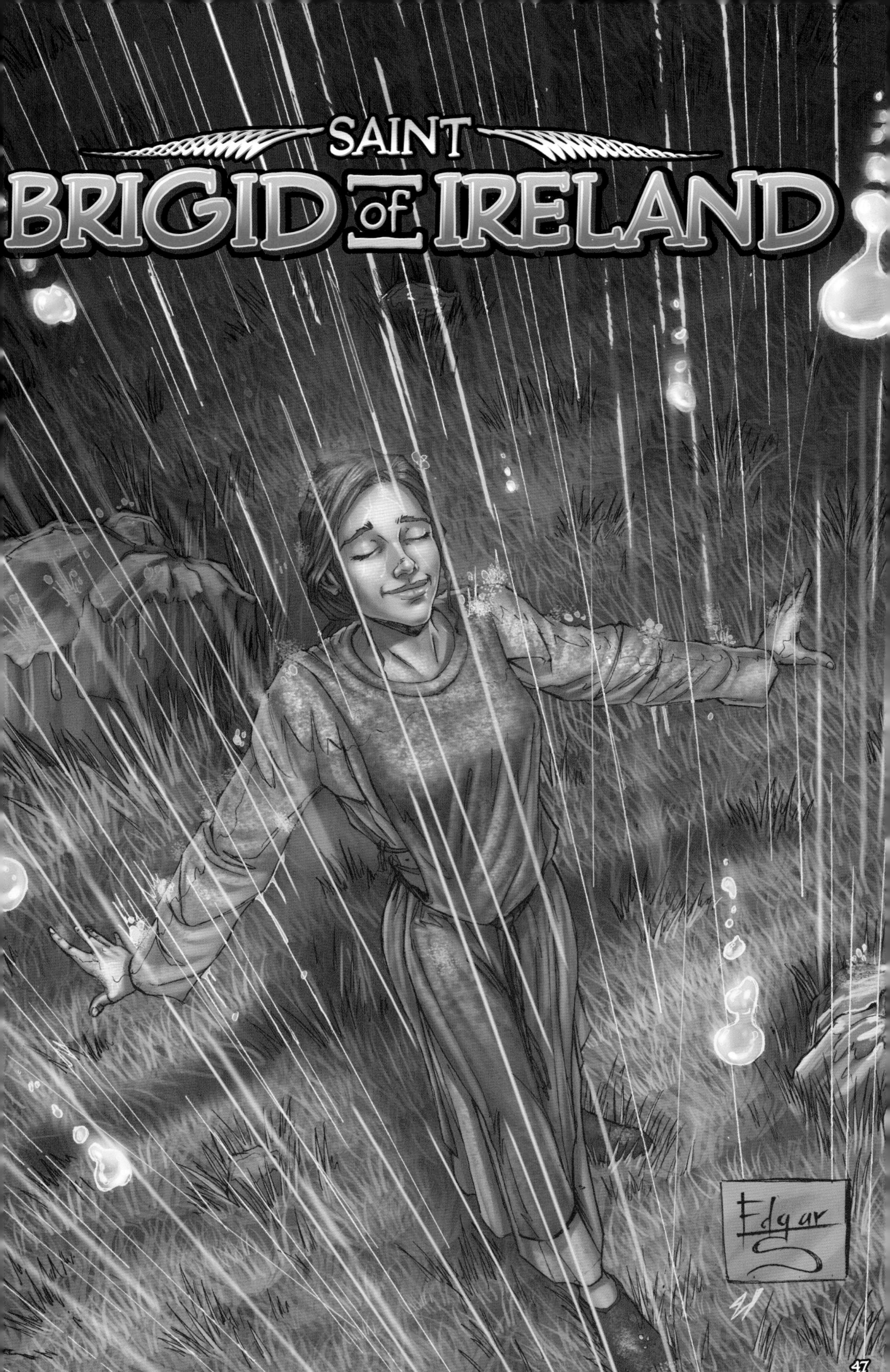
SAINT
BRIGID of IRELAND
Edgar

SAINT BRIGID OF IRELAND

St. Brigid of Ireland's tale is as multifaceted as her following. She is often known as **St. Bride**, Mary of the Gael, and the **Patroness of Ireland.** Beloved for her **charity,** kindness, and the founding of many **convents,** monasteries, and schools, St. Brigid is also associated with **St. Patrick,** the other **Patron Saint of Ireland.** Both were avid leaders in the **conversion** of Ireland's **pagan** worshippers to followers of Christ. During her life, St. Brigid wove a cross made of rushes to symbolize Christ's **death** and **resurrection.** To this day, many who love St. Brigid wear or display the **cross of St. Brigid** in honor of her life.

Born in **fifth century Ireland,** there is much we do not know about this **beloved saint.** However, all biographers agree that this Lady of Ireland led a most **extraordinary life.**

Producer: Daniel Burton   **Editorial:** Kimberly Black

Story: Jen Murvin Edwards   **Pencils:** Edgar Salazar   **Colors:** Ulises Palomera   **Letters:** Keith Bahrenburg

Designs: Keith Bahrenburg & Adam Buechler

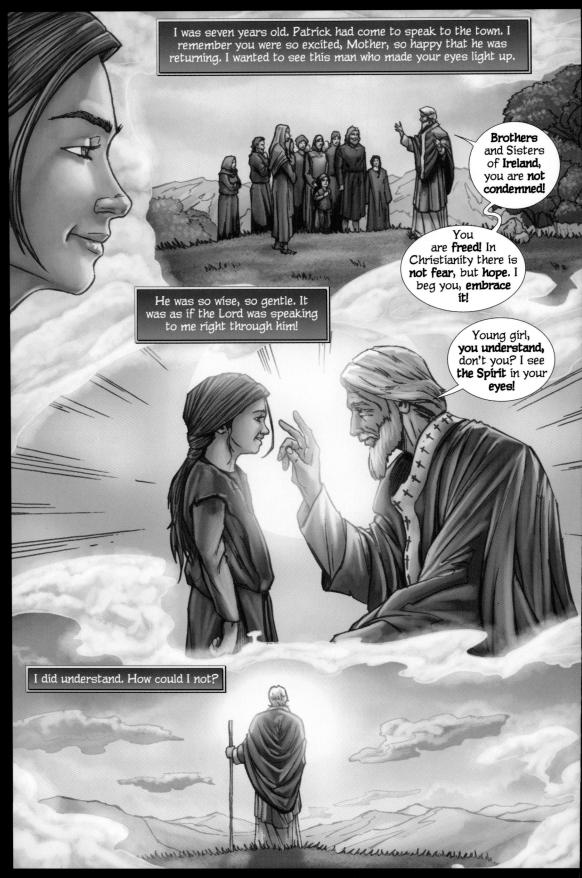

Brigid, there you are! I was so worried.

I can't do it.

You what? You can't --

Mother, you understand, don't you? I am a Christian! I long to dedicate my life to the Lord ... and to no one else.

You never had that choice, Mother. You were a slave.

I only wish to have the freedom my Lord has given me!

The only master I have now is the Lord. My life will be spent serving Him.

I just have to figure out how!

St. Brigid went on to found several other convents, and she made Kildare into a double monastery where nuns and monks could serve and study. St. Brigid governed this institution along with St. Conleth. She later went on to establish a school of arts, teaching skills such as metal working and manuscript illumination.

The flame she had dedicated to Christ was maintained by her followers until Henry VIII's forces destroyed it during the sixteenth century.

St. Brigid contributed greatly to the spread of Christianity in Ireland. She served the Lord and remained faithful to her vows for the rest of her days.

St. Brigid is known as the Patroness of Ireland and the patron saint of dairy maids, nuns, scholars, and travelers. Her feast day is celebrated on February 1.

A Saint's Journey

✻ **c. 451** Brigid is born at Faughart, Ireland, to her father Dubhthach and mother Brocca.

✻ Inspired by the preaching of St. Patrick from an early age, Brigid endeavores to live a life of service. She often gives suffering souls whatever she finds, even when it angers her father.

✻ Tired of Brigid's **generosity**, her **father** finally lets Brigid go after **she gives** to a leper his jewel-encrusted sword. Brigid also gives away much of the milk at the dairy farm where **her mother** is enslaved. Nevertheless, the farm prospers, and the Druid owner frees her mother.

✻ Once Brigid takes her vows and dedicates her life to Christ, she founds her first convent in Clara.

✻ **c. 470** Brigid founds and becomes abbess of a double monastery for both monks and nuns at Cill-Dara, now known as **Kildare.** **Kildare** becomes so important to the **Catholic** faith in **Ireland** that, for **many** years, **St. Brigid** is considered **superioress general** for **all convents** in the country.

✻ **c. 525** Brigid dies at Kildare.

✻ In **honor** of St. Brigid's **place of birth, Faughart Church** is founded by **St. Morienna.**

✻ The **cross of St. Brigid** is a **woven cross** made of **rushes** to symbolize Christ's death and **resurrection.**

✻ Brigid's childhood **water well,** depicted on the first page of this story, is known to this day as **"St. Brigid's Well"** and is a **destination** in Faughart for many **pilgrims.** Many other wells across Ireland are dedicated

Who is your spiritual mentor?

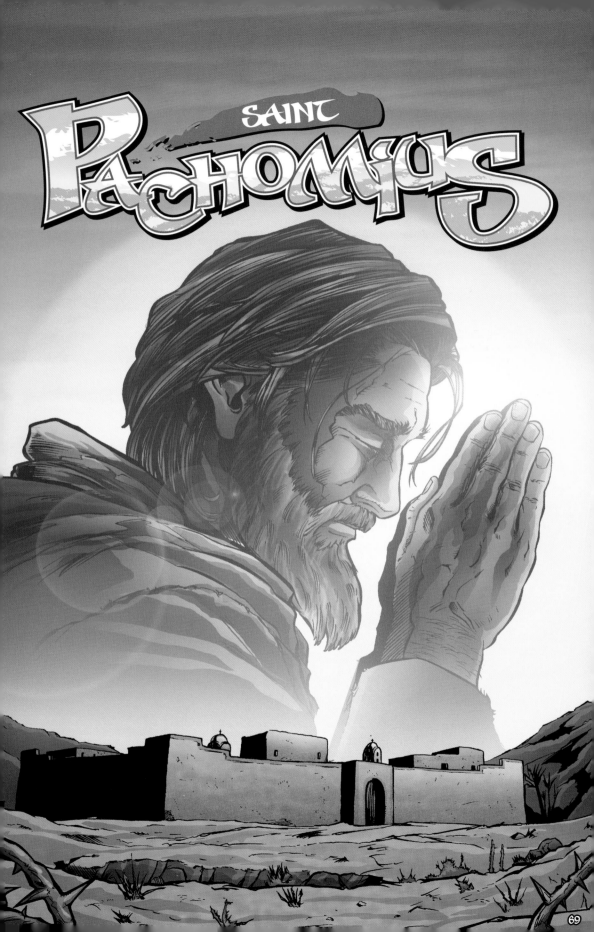

SAINT PACHOMIUS

STORY:

JEN MURVIN EDWARDS & ROGER BROWN

PENCILS:

EDGAR SALAZAR

INKS:

GENARO OLAVARRIETA

COLORS:

CARSTEN BRADLEY

LETTERS & DESIGN:

KEITH BAHRENBURG

ADDITIONAL DESIGN:

ADAM BUECHLER

PRODUCER:

DANIEL BURTON

EDITORIAL:

KIMBERLY BLACK

INTRODUCTION:

TWO THOUSAND YEARS AGO, ST. PACHOMIUS WAS BORN IN THE UPPER THEBAID OF EGYPT. AS THE YEARS PASSED AND PACHOMIUS GREW UP, HE BECAME A SOLDIER IN THE ARMY OF THE EMPEROR CONSTANTINE. WHILE PACHOMIUS WAS LIVING AN EXCITING LIFE IN THE ARMY, HE FOUND THAT IT WAS ALSO EMPTY. AT THE YOUNG AGE OF TWENTY-THREE, PACHOMIUS BEGAN SEARCHING FOR PURPOSE AND PASSION.

ST. PACHOMIUS' SEARCH FOR FAITH AND TRUTH LED HIM ON AN INCREDIBLE JOURNEY. IN THE DESERT, THIS SPECIAL MAN FOUND THE LORD -- AND WITH GOD AT HIS SIDE, PACHOMIUS SPREAD CHRIST'S MESSAGE THROUGHOUT THE LANDS OF EGYPT. ALTHOUGH HE MET MANY OBSTACLES ALONG THE WAY, HIS FAITH REMAINED STRONG, AS DID HIS MESSAGE OF HOPE.

ST. PACHOMIUS' STORY CAN TEACH US ABOUT GOD'S PLAN FOR OUR LIVES. AS GOD WORKED THROUGH THIS SAINT IN THE HOT SANDS OF EGYPT, SO, TOO, HE CAN GIVE US DIRECTION, HOPE, AND PURPOSE. SAINT PACHOMIUS' FEAST DAY IS MAY 9.

THIS WAS *MY SHIP*.

WELL, MAYBE NOT *MINE*, EXACTLY, THOUGH I *CALLED* IT HOME FOR *MANY YEARS*. IT BELONGED TO *THE ARMY*.

YOU SEE, I WAS A *SOLDIER* BEFORE I -- *WAIT*, I SHOULD NOT GET AHEAD OF MYSELF.

MY NAME IS *PACHOMIUS*, AND *THIS* IS MY STORY.

IT *STARTED* ON *THIS DAY* YEARS AGO, WHEN I WAS *ONLY A YOUNG MAN*. I WAS A SOLDIER TRANSPORTING PRISONERS *ON THE SEA*.

LITTLE DID I *KNOW* THAT ON THIS DAY MY *LIFE* WOULD *CHANGE*.

FOREVER.

MY FRIEND WAS *RIGHT*. THE OLD SERVER *HAD* SPARKED MY *INTEREST* AND, A *CURIOUS* MAN AT HEART, I *COULDN'T* LET HIM GO UNTIL I UNDERSTOOD WHAT *HIS WORDS MEANT*.

I *SOUGHT* THE OLD MAN ...

NOT KNOWING AS I DID SO THAT I SOUGHT SOMETHING ELSE *ENTIRELY*.

YOU ARE A *DETERMINED* MAN, *PACHOMIUS!* SURELY GOD HAS *INSPIRED* YOU TO *SEEK* HIM SO *PASSIONATELY*.

SIR, I AM *NOT* SEARCHING FOR *GOD* AS *MUCH* AS THE *MEANING* BEHIND YOUR *WORDS* ...

AND *THOSE* ARE ONE AND THE SAME, MY *YOUNG FRIEND*. FOR BEHIND ALL WORDS, ALL JOY, *ALL LOVE* IN MY LIFE *SITS GOD* IN HIS *WISDOM* AND *MERCY*.

HERE, I WILL *SHOW YOU*.

AND SO I *READ*.

I READ AS I *NEVER* READ *BEFORE*, AS ONE WOULD READ THE *SWEET WORDS* OF A *LOVE* LETTER...

IN THE *WORD* OF GOD, I FOUND MUCH MORE THAN I *EVER* DREAMED.

TO READ *ALL* NIGHT TAKES MUCH *DEVOTION*, BROTHER.

YOU ARE TRULY A *MESSENGER*, AND I HAVE RECEIVED MY *CALLING*.

I WISH TO BE *BAPTIZED AT ONCE!*

THE OLD MAN *TOLD* ME OF THE CEREMONY AND OF *THE SACRAMENTS* I WOULD RECEIVE AND OF THEIR *MEANING*.

I WILL BE *PREPARED* THIS AFTERNOON. UNTIL THEN, *I WILL PRAY*.

AND -- *THANK YOU*, FRIEND.

FOR THANKFUL *I WAS*.

AS THE *SUN* SET OVER THE *NILE RIVER* IN THE EGYPTIAN SKY, I *PREPARED* TO BE *BAPTIZED* INTO CHRIST.

COME, YOUNG MAN, IT IS *TIME*.

I *BELIEVE*.

AS THE *HEAVENLY HOSTS* DO WHEN *ANY* SON OR DAUGHTER IS BROUGHT INTO *THE FOLD*, THEY *REJOICED*.

I COULD ALMOST *HEAR* THEM IN THE *LAPPING* OF THE RIVER AS I SAID *THE WORDS*.

THE *MONTHS* PASSED *QUICKLY* ...

PACHOMIUS, WHERE ARE YOU *GOING*?

GOOD FRIEND, I FEEL THE LORD *CALLING ME* INTO THE DESERTS OF EGYPT ... THOUGH FOR WHAT PURPOSE I HAVE *YET* TO *KNOW.*

YOU SURELY PAY HEED TO GOD'S *WILL,* FOR *ONLY* TODAY I HEARD THE TOWNSPEOPLE SPEAK OF A MAN NAMED *PALAEMON.*

HE LIVES IN THE DESERT AND IS *KNOWN* AS THE *MOST HOLY* OF MEN.

GO, PACHOMIUS.

THE DESERT AWAITS.

THE DESERT IS A *SHIFTY CREATURE.*

IN *ONE MOMENT* THE SAND CAN *CHANGE* FROM A CALM, *YELLOW SEA* TO A WILD *BEAST,* THE WIND WHIPPING THE GRAINS AGAINST *YOUR SKIN AND MOUTH.*

I *KNEW* THAT TO SURVIVE, I HAD TO TRUST IN *GOD.*

WITH *HIM* AT THE *HELM,* INTO THE *DESERT* I RODE.

FOR *DAYS* I SAW NOTHING BUT *SAND AND SKY* AND THE *BACK* OF MY CAMEL AS I HEADED TOWARD *MY DESTINY.*

UNTIL FINALLY, I SAW THEM -- *NOMADS.*

FRIENDS! I SEEK THE HERMIT *PALAEMON!*

YOU ARE *CLOSE,* TRAVELER! JUST *OVER THE RIDGE* THERE AND *EAST!*

YOU MUST RIDE *QUICKLY,* FOR THE AIR IS DANGEROUS *THIS NIGHT!*

INDEED IT *WAS.* AS *NIGHT FELL,* THE *SANDSTORM* WHIPPED AND *WAILED,* AND I STRUGGLED TO *FIND THE WAY.*

MY *NOSTRILS* FILLED WITH *SAND,* AND I COVERED MY *MOUTH* WITH MY *SHAWL* IN ORDER TO *BREATHE ...*

BUT THE *LORD* WAS WITH ME. AND THE WINDS *CALMED.*

I HAD *SURVIVED.*

FINALLY, I ARRIVED. I HAD *FOUND HIM* --

PALAEMON.

I *SAW* THIS HOLY MAN DEEP IN *PRAYER.*

AS I *SOUGHT* TO *QUIET* MYSELF AND THE CAMEL WHO HAD *CARRIED* ME SO MANY MILES ...

I *KNEW* WHAT I *MUST DO.*

WELCOME, BROTHER.

PALAEMON'S *TEACHINGS* BEGAN AT ONCE.

YOU *KNOW* HOW THE DESERT *CAN* BE --

YES, LIKE THE *SANDSTORM?*

NOT *JUST* THE SANDSTORM, MY FRIEND. OH NO --

THE DESERT *CAN* BE SNEAKY, *DANGEROUS* WHEN YOU LEAST *EXPECT* IT.

SOME PLANTS *LOOK* HARMLESS ...

BUT A *SMALL PIECE* OF THEM CAN KILL A MAN IN AN *INSTANT.*

THERE ARE *ALSO* PLANTS THAT CAN *HEAL* --

THESE I WILL SHOW YOU.

THE DESERT *CAN BE* YOUR *FRIEND,* BUT YOU MUST RESPECT IT AT *ALL TIMES.*

THANK YOU, PALAEMON. BETWEEN YOUR *LESSONS* ABOUT *THE LORD* AND *THOSE* OF THE DESERT, I HAVE *LEARNED MORE* IN THE LAST FEW DAYS THAN IN MY WHOLE *LIFETIME.*

TIME PASSED AND WITH IT, *MY IGNORANCE.*

PALAEMON, IS SOMETHING *WRONG?* YOU HAVEN'T SAID A WORD *ALL MORNING.*

I HAVE BEEN *PRAYING,* BROTHER. IT'S TIME FOR *YOU* TO GO OUT ON YOUR *OWN* ...

FACE THE *DESERT* WITH CHRIST AS *YOUR GUIDE* AND RESCUER --

I SHALL AWAIT *YOUR RETURN!*

Take this scroll, Pachomius ...

You are to build a monastery.

BUT -- BUT WHERE? HERE? TELL ME, PLEASE --

You will know where to build -- the Lord will speak to your heart, and you will listen.

YES. I VOW MY SERVICE TO GOD!

THE VISION SHOOK ME TO MY BONES, AND I ACHED WITH SHAME IN THE LIGHT OF THE PRESENCE OF THIS ANGEL FROM GOD!

AS I RODE, THE BLOOD RACED IN MY VEINS, AND I PRAYED MORE FERVENTLY THAN I HAD EVER PRAYED BEFORE -- PRAISING GOD OVER AND OVER FOR THE INCREDIBLE GIFT HE HAD GIVEN ME --

THIS TASK HE HAD GIVEN TO ME.

PACHOMIUS, HAVE YOU RETURNED ALREADY?

PALAEMON! MY BROTHER! COME -- COME AND GREET ME! I HAVE MUCH TO TELL YOU!

THIS VISION IS **SURELY** FROM GOD. WE MUST **EXAMINE** THE SCROLL **IMMEDIATELY!**

PLANS, GUIDES -- I LOOK AT **THESE DOCUMENTS** AND KNOW I MUST BUILD **THE MONASTERY** AT TABENNISI.

IF **THAT** IS WHAT IS IN YOUR **HEART**, THEN YES, PACHOMIUS. **TABENNISI** IS WHERE IT **WILL STAND.**

THIS DESERT HAS BEEN **YOUR COMPANION** FOR A LONG TIME, BUT --

I WAS **HOPING** --

IF **YOU** COULD --

THERE IS NO NEED TO **ASK.** OF COURSE I WILL **JOIN YOU** IN THIS MISSION.

WE PRAISED THE **LORD** AND **PRAYED** FOR **HIS** GUIDANCE.

ALTHOUGH WE WERE **LEAVING** THE DESERT AND ITS **MANY** THREATS ...

WE **WERE** ENTERING A NEW WORLD WITH **NEW DANGERS.**

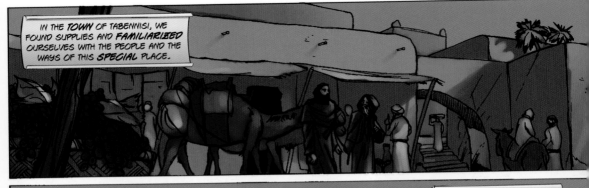

IN THE *TOWN* OF TABENNISI, WE FOUND SUPPLIES AND *FAMILIARIZED* OURSELVES WITH THE PEOPLE AND THE WAYS OF THIS *SPECIAL* PLACE.

AS THE *DAYS* PASSED, WE THANKED GOD, SIDE *BY SIDE*, FOR HIS *GUIDANCE*, MERCY, *AND GRACE*.

THE *WORK* OF THE LORD IS *JUST THAT* --

WORK.

AT *THE END* OF EACH DAY WE SAT ON SORE LIMBS AND *SMILED* --

FOR *ALREADY* HIS HOUSE WAS TAKING *SHAPE*.

THE LORD **SPOKE** TO ME **DAILY** THROUGH THE VILLAGERS, HIS PLAN COMING **FULL CIRCLE**.

WE'VE SEEN YOU **BUILD** --

AND **YET** YOU WILL EARN **NO MONEY** FROM THIS **ENDEAVOR?**

WE **DON'T** UNDERSTAND.

I KNOW ALL TOO WELL YOUR **CONFUSION**, BROTHERS. COME, AND LET ME **TELL YOU** WHY WE **WORK** FOR NO PAY.

THE LORD **BROUGHT** US MANY MEN -- HIS WALLS ROSE BY THE SWEAT OF **HIS FOLLOWERS.**

BUT AS **WE BUILT** THIS MONASTERY-- A PLACE FOR LEARNING, **PRAYER**, AND **CHRIST-LIKE LIVING** -- I SENSED AN UNEASINESS IN MY FRIEND **PALAEMON.**

PALAEMON, I **MUST** SPEAK WITH YOU **AT ONCE.**

BROTHER, WILL *YOU* LET ME EASE THE *ANGUISH* I'VE *SEEN* IN YOUR EYES OVER THESE *LAST FEW WEEKS?*

THE *LORD* IS WITH YOU --

AND YOU WILL *ALWAYS* BE IN MY *PRAYERS.*

AS *ALWAYS,* PACHOMIUS, YOU ARE *OBSERVANT.* I HAVE BEEN RESTLESS. THE DESERT *CALLS* ME HOME.

I *WAS* HOPING THIS DAY *MIGHT* NEVER COME --

OR AT LEAST WHEN IT *DID,* I WOULD BE *READY.*

I *DON'T KNOW* HOW TO SAY GOODBYE, *OLD FRIEND.*

PALAEMON *RETURNED* TO THE DESERT.

I *NEVER* SAW HIM AGAIN.

THE WORLD *KEPT SPINNING,* AND *WITH IT,* THE WORK GOD HAD *ENTRUSTED* TO ME.

I USED MY *KNOWLEDGE* OF DESERT *PLANTS* TO *TREAT* THE SICK *AMONG* US, AND I TRAINED MY BROTHERS IN THE WAYS OF *MEDICINE.*

REMEMBERING HOW THE WORDS OF THE *LORD* HAD TOUCHED *MY SOUL,* I SOUGHT TO *BRING* THOSE *SAME WORDS* TO MANY *OTHERS* ACROSS THE LAND.

BUT IT WAS *NOT OVER YET* ...

BROTHER PACHOMIUS, I *MUST* SPEAK WITH YOU *AT ONCE*.

BROTHERS, OUR *NUMBERS* ARE GROWING *QUICKLY*, AND THERE IS ONLY *ONE SOLUTION*!

A *SECOND MONASTERY* WAS BUILT SWIFTLY, FOR WE HAD LEARNED FROM OUR *PAST MISTAKES*.

AFTER IT WAS *COMPLETED*, WE KEPT *BUILDING* UNTIL A TOTAL OF *NINE* MONASTERIES *DOTTED* THE DESERT, *FILLED* WITH MEN *SEEKING THE LORD*.

MY *SISTER MARIA JOINED* OUR WORK, AND WITH MY HELP *TWO NUNNERIES* WERE *ADDED* TO *GOD'S* SERVICE.

YES, ALL SEEMED WELL FOR *MANY YEARS*.

AS IN THE *DESERT*, IN *LIFE* A STORM CAN STRIKE WHEN YOU *LEAST EXPECT* IT.

BROTHER -- WE NEED YOUR *HELP!*

NOT *ENOUGH* FOOD? HOW CAN *THIS* BE?

LORD, *WHY?* AFTER *ALL WE'VE DONE* ...

DOUBT IS *NATURAL*, FRIENDS, IN *TIMES OF NEED.* I *DESPAIRED* ONLY FOR A MOMENT, AND THEN I REMEMBERED ...

GOD'S WORD SAYS, "*ASK* AND YE *SHALL* RECEIVE, *SEEK* AND YE SHALL *FIND*."

AND SO I *PRAYED* FOR A SOLUTION.

WAKE UP, BROTHER --

COME AND *SEE.*

THE *LORD'S PLAN* MAY NOT *ALWAYS* BE OUR OWN, BUT IN THIS *INSTANCE,* HE SENT US *A MIRACLE.*

THE PEOPLE OF THE *VILLAGE* HEARD OF OUR PLIGHT AND *DONATED BREAD* TO THE *MONASTERIES!*

PRAISE *THE LORD,* BROTHER, FOR HE HAS *HEARD OUR PRAYER.* I WILL GO AND *TELL THE OTHERS.*

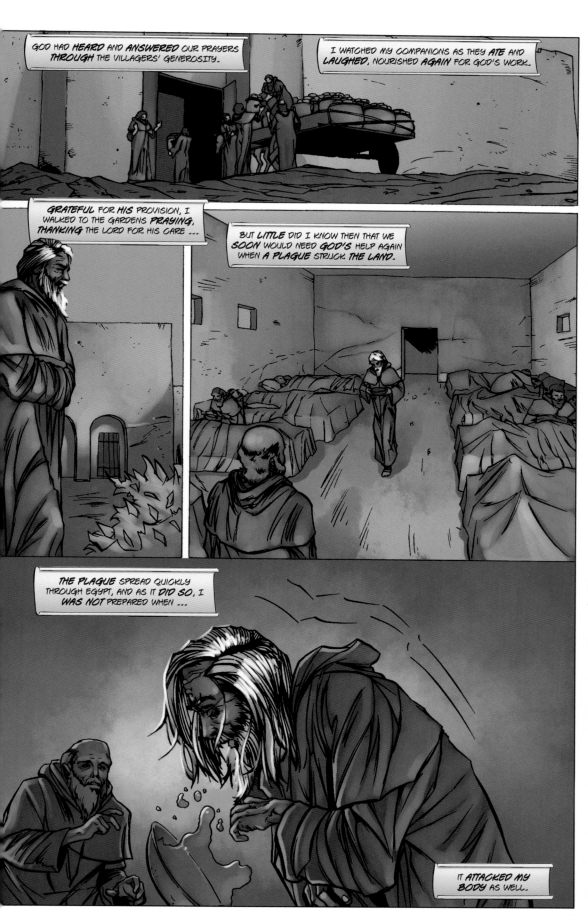

GOD HAD **HEARD** AND **ANSWERED** OUR PRAYERS **THROUGH** THE VILLAGERS' GENEROSITY.

I WATCHED MY COMPANIONS AS THEY **ATE** AND **LAUGHED**, NOURISHED **AGAIN** FOR GOD'S WORK.

GRATEFUL FOR **HIS** PROVISION, I WALKED TO THE GARDENS **PRAYING**, **THANKING** THE LORD FOR HIS CARE ...

BUT **LITTLE** DID I KNOW THEN THAT WE **SOON** WOULD NEED **GOD'S** HELP AGAIN WHEN **A PLAGUE** STRUCK **THE LAND**.

THE PLAGUE SPREAD QUICKLY THROUGH EGYPT, AND AS IT **DID SO**, I **WAS NOT** PREPARED WHEN ...

IT **ATTACKED MY BODY** AS WELL.

BEFORE I LEAVE *THIS EARTH*, I WANT TO *PRAY* FOR MY *FRIEND*, PALAEMON, OUT IN *THE DESERT* AND *WISH* HIM *PEACE* AND *JOY.*

I WANT TO *PRAY* FOR THE *MONASTERIES* AND NUNNERIES THAT *THEIR WORK* GLORIFIES *GOD* AND THAT THEY *CONTINUE* TO FLOURISH AFTER I JOIN MY *FATHER IN HEAVEN* ...

AS *MY HEART* BEATS *SLOWLY*, I FEEL DEEPLY IN MY *BONES* THE *PEACE* OF *MY FATHER'S* LOVE AND MERCY.

MAY *ALL* WHO HEAR *HIS NAME* FIND *LOVE* AND *MERCY.*

PACHOMIUS'S TEACHINGS AND *RULES* FOR LIVING A *COMMUNAL* AND MONASTIC LIFE *LIVED ON* LONG AFTER HIS *PASSING.* THE MONASTERIES HE *FOUNDED* WOULD STILL HOUSE THE FAITHFUL *SEVEN CENTURIES LATER.*

A Saint's Journey

C. 292
PACHOMIUS IS BORN IN THEBES.

C. 312
PACHOMIUS ENLISTS IN THE ROMAN ARMY. WHILE IN THE ARMY, LOCAL CHRISTIANS BRING FOOD AND PROVISIONS TO HIM AND HIS MEN. THESE KIND ACTS FOREVER LEAVE AN IMPRESSION ON THE YOUNG PACHOMIUS.

C. 314
AFTER LEAVING THE ARMY, PACHOMIUS IS CONVERTED AND BAPTIZED.

C. 317
PACHOMIUS SEEKS OUT THE WISDOM AND GUIDANCE OF THE HERMIT PALAEMON.

C. 318-347
PACHOMIUS SETS OUT TO ORGANIZE MONASTERIES OF MEN IN THE DESERTS OF TABENNISI, EGYPT. SOON, OVER ONE-HUNDRED MEN JOIN HIS MONASTERY.

C. 348
HE REMAINS ABBOT FOR FORTY YEARS UNTIL HE APPOINTS A SUCCESSOR BEFORE HIS DEATH.

TODAY
ST. PACHOMIUS IS REGARDED AS THE FOUNDER OF CENOBITIC MONASTICISM, WHICH STRESSES COMMUNITY LIFE OVER A LIFE OF SOLITUDE, WHICH IS CALLED EREMITIC MONASTICISM.

How do you measure strength?

Saint Anne Line

ANNE LINE WAS A DEVOTED CATHOLIC. THE PRICE OF HER FAITH WAS *GREAT*. SHE LIVED IN *ENGLAND* DURING THE *SIXTEENTH CENTURY*, A TIME WHEN IT WAS AGAINST THE LAW TO *BE CATHOLIC.* IN FACT, BEING CATHOLIC WAS CONSIDERED *TREASON.*

BUT STILL, ANNE *BELIEVED.*

HER FATHER *DISOWNED* HER. HER *HUSBAND* WAS *THROWN OUT* OF THE COUNTRY. SHE WAS FORCED, AGAIN AND AGAIN, TO *FLEE* IN THE MIDDLE OF *THE NIGHT*, ONE STEP AHEAD OF BEING ARRESTED. SHE FACED TORTURE, *IMPRISONMENT*, EVEN A *DEATH SENTENCE.*

BUT STILL, ANNE *BELIEVED.*

Producer: DANIEL BURTON

Editorial: KIMBERLY BLACK

Story: TERRY COLLINS

Pencils: SERGIO CARIELLO

Colors: DANIEL BURTON

Letters / Designs: KEITH BAHRENBURG

Additional Designs: ADAM BUECHLER

GOD, THEY *THINK* THEY CAN *IMPRISON ME.*

THESE MEN HAVE *LOCKED* ME IN A CELL, HELD ME WITHOUT PROPER *FOOD,* DENIED ME CLEAN *WATER* --

TO TRY TO *BREAK ME.*

YET, I AM *UNBROKEN.*

YOU KEEP ME *WHOLE.*

THEY *BELIEVE* MY PHYSICAL SICKNESS IS A SIGN OF *WEAKNESS.*

THEY ARE *WRONG.*

THE OLD BAILEY COURT. LONDON, ENGLAND.

THESE *JAILERS*, THESE *JUDGES*, THESE SO-CALLED *RULERS* OF MEN --

THEY *DO NOT* THINK I WILL *SURVIVE* THIS *ORDEAL*.

FATHER, WE ARE **NOT ASKING** FOR YOUR PERMISSION. YOU SEE, WE HAVE **ALREADY CONVERTED** TO CATHOLICISM.

DO YOU **REALIZE** WHAT YOU HAVE DONE? IF THIS **GETS OUT** -- OUR FAMILY IS **RUINED!**

BEING CATHOLIC IS AN **ACT OF TREASON** AGAINST THE GOVERNMENT!

I **WONDERED** WHY YOU HAD STOPPED ATTENDING **SERVICES** AT THE **CHURCH** OF ENGLAND. YOU'VE FALLEN IN WITH SINNERS -- **CRIMINALS!**

ANNE, YOU'LL SEND US ALL TO THE **GALLOWS!**

YOU'LL BE CHARGED WITH **RECUSANCY!** * ARRESTED AND JAILED!

I WILL **NOT ALLOW** THIS FOOLISHNESS TO DESTROY THE HEIGHAM **FAMILY NAME!**

FATHER, **PLEASE!**

LEAVE THIS HOUSE! LEAVE NOW, AND NEVER **RETURN!**

*RECUSANCY: THE CRIME OF REFUSING TO ATTEND THE MANDATORY SERVICES OF THE CHURCH OF ENGLAND.

BUT THOUGH *MY FATHER* HAD DISOWNED US, I MANAGED TO FIND A *RAY OF LIGHT* IN THE DARKNESS OF *MY WORLD* -- AND ONLY FOUR YEARS LATER, *I MARRIED HIM.*

ANNE? ARE YOU *LISTENING* TO ME?

OF COURSE, *MR. LINE.*

FOR A MOMENT, I *SAW WORRY* CLOUD THE FACE OF *MY BEAUTIFUL WIFE.*

GOD HAS GIVEN US A *GLORIOUS* DAY TO ENJOY. WE'LL HAVE *NO BAD THOUGHTS.*

I'M SORRY, ROGER. I WAS THINKING OF MY *FATHER* --

I WISH HE *COULD* HAVE *SEEN* US JOINED IN *MATRIMONY.*

YOUR FATHER, SITTING THROUGH A *CATHOLIC WEDDING?* SURELY YOU *JEST!*

I *MISS* HIM, ROGER. I MISS HAVING *A FAMILY.*

EVEN THOUGH WE ARE NOW *WED*, THERE ARE NIGHTS WHEN I FEEL *SO ALONE* IN THE WORLD.

SOON, MY DEAR, WE SHALL HAVE *OUR OWN FAMILY* TO LOVE.

HOW CAN WE THINK OF SUCH *THINGS?* BOTH OF US ARE *CRIMINALS* IN THE EYES OF *ENGLAND.*

BUT *NOT* IN THE EYES OF *GOD.*

I *PROMISE* YOU, *OUR* CHILDREN WILL BE RAISED TO *WORSHIP FREELY* AND *WITHOUT FEAR.*

YOU'RE *NOT ALONE,* DEAR, SWEET ANNE. I'LL ALWAYS BE *HERE* FOR YOU.

WITHIN A *MONTH*, ROGER WAS *IMPRISONED* FOR RECUSANCY. BEATEN, TORTURED, *BROKEN* -- HE NEVER UTTERED A *SINGLE WORD*.

BEING *BORN* TO A FAMILY OF INFLUENCE *SAVED HIS LIFE*.

THE JUSTICES WERE *MERCIFUL*. HE WAS ALLOWED TO GO *ABROAD* TO FLANDERS, *NEVER TO RETURN*.

OUR *MARRIAGE VOWS* WERE *NEVER* RECOGNIZED BY THE ENGLISH COURTS AS THEY WERE TAKEN *IN SECRET*, IN A *CATHOLIC CEREMONY*.

I *NEVER* SAW *MY HUSBAND* AGAIN.

SOON AFTER, MY *HEALTH* BEGAN TO *FAIL*. I WAS *WEAK*, UNABLE TO *WALK* OR *EVEN BREATHE* ON DAYS WHEN MY ILLNESS WAS AT *ITS WORST*.

BUT *INSIDE*, I WAS AS *STRONG* AS OAK.

ROGER *WAS* RIGHT. I WAS *NOT ALONE*. GOD WAS *WITH* ME -- THEN, NOW, AND *ALWAYS*.

AND BY *TAKING* MY HUSBAND FROM MY ARMS, *GOD* HAD SHOWN ME *THE PATH* I WAS *DESTINED* TO FOLLOW.

MY LIFE HAD *MEANING* -- TO *HELP* MY *FELLOW CATHOLICS.*

I *TRAVELED* TO THE TOWN OF *BRADDOX* TO ASSIST A *MRS. WISEMAN* WITH A *SAFE HOUSE.*

SHE WAS ONE OF THE *KINDEST WOMEN* I *EVER MET,* AND I *NEVER* EVEN *KNEW* HER *FIRST NAME!*

CATHOLICS WERE SEEING THEIR LANDS *TAKEN,* THEIR BUSINESSES *CONFISCATED,* AND THEY HAD *NOWHERE TO TURN* FOR HELP.

SHE OFFERED *SANCTUARY* WITHIN *HER* WALLS. *ALL* WHO BELIEVED *WERE WELCOME.*

FOR *MONTHS,* WORD *SPREAD* AMONG THE FAITHFUL, AND OUR CONGREGATION *GREW.*

PERHAPS OUR *PRIDE* IN SUCH GROWTH WAS OUR *DOWNFALL.* MRS. WISEMAN WAS *ARRESTED.*

HER *CRIME* OF PROTECTING CATHOLICS COULD EARN BUT *ONE PUNISHMENT*:

DEATH.

WITH HER PASSING, THE *HOUSE* I'D GROWN TO LOVE WAS *BURNED TO ASHES*.

THE *TIME* HAD ARRIVED FOR *MY JOURNEY* TO *CONTINUE*.

MRS. WISEMAN HAD TOLD ME OF A *JESUIT PRIEST* IN LONDON WHO RAN A *SAFE HOUSE* FOR *CLERGY*.

HIS NAME WAS *FATHER JOHN GERARD*.

IN *1597, HE* WAS *CAPTURED* AND HELD WITHIN THE WALLS OF THE *ACCURSED* TOWER OF LONDON. I ASSUMED *HIS DUTIES* IN THE HOUSE.

I *PROVIDED* FOOD, HOPE, AND SANCTUARY FOR MY *FELLOW CATHOLICS*.

UNLIKE POOR MRS. WISEMAN, *FATHER GERARD* WAS *NOT* WITHOUT *ALLIES*. HE WAS ABLE TO ESCAPE *BEFORE* BEING *KILLED*.

WITH HIS FLIGHT, HIS *HOMES* WERE *SEIZED*. FOR THE FIRST TIME, *MY NAME* APPEARED WITHIN THE *BOOKS* OF *THE COURT OF ENGLAND*.

THEY HAD *NO PROOF*, BUT PROOF MATTERED *LITTLE*. A SOVEREIGN WOULD PAY FOR A *NUMBER* OF *WITNESSES*.

AGAIN, I WAS *FORCED* TO RUN FOR *MY LIFE*.

GOD, SOME NIGHTS I *DREAM* --

I DREAM OF *MY FATHER*, LOST TO *HATRED*. I KNOW YOU WILL *RECEIVE* HIM.

I *AWAKEN*, AND THINK OF *MY HUSBAND*, STOLEN AWAY. *TAKE CARE* OF HIM.

I *WONDER* ABOUT MY POOR BROTHER *WILLIAM*. KEEP HIM *SAFE*.

THANK YOU FOR ALLOWING ME TO RECEIVE *YOUR GRACE*.

I AM *READY*, GOD.

MY WORK HERE IS *FINISHED*.

ON *FEBRUARY 27, 1601*, ANNE LINE W HANGED ON THE SCAFFOLD OF *TYBU* OUTSIDE *NEWGATE PRISON*. BEFORE B *BLINDFOLDED*, SHE *KISSED* THE GALLO

A Saint's Journey

-- c. 1565 --
Anne Heigham is born into a wealthy and respected British family.

-- c. 1580 --
Anne and her younger brother William are both disowned by their father for their Catholic beliefs.

--- 1583 ---
At the age of nineteen, Anne Heigham marries a fellow Catholic, Roger Line.

--- 1585 ---
Roger Line is arrested for his refusal to give up his Catholicism. Though he escapes death, he is exiled to Flanders.

--- 1586 ---
Inspired by Roger's suffering and seeing her pathway in the service of the Lord, Anne becomes active in the underground Catholic Church in England.

--- 1594 ---
Roger Line dies as a disinherited and broken man in Flanders.

--- 1597 ---
Anne assumes responsibility for a Catholic safe house when Father John Gerard is captured and imprisoned. By the end of the year, Anne is on the run again from the authorities.

--- 1601 ---
Arrested on Candlemas Day for holding Mass, Anne is sentenced to execution by the Court of England. She is taken to the gallows and hanged on February 27th.

--- 1929 ---
On December 15th, Anne is declared blessed by Pope Pius XI

--- 1970 ---
On October 25th, Pope Paul VI canonizes Anne as one of the Forty Martyrs of England and Wales.

GO!
Make
disciples
of all
nations.

Baptize them in the name of the Father, the Son, and the Holy Spirit.

Teach them to obey everything I have commanded you.

Matthew
28:19-20a